I0011088

Safeguarding
Your
Retirement

Safeguarding Your Retirement

11 Key Steps

*To Protect and Grow
Your Retirement Account*

Jack D. Howell Jr.

The American Institute
For Financial Education

Copyright © 2003-2005 by Jack D. Howell, Jr.

All Rights reserved.

No part of this book may be reproduced or transmitted in any form or by any means, electronic or mechanical, including photocopying, recording, or by any other information storage and retrieval system, without the permission in writing from the publisher, except in the case of brief quotations embodied in articles or reviews written for inclusion in a magazine, newspaper, or broadcast.

Published in the United States of America by:

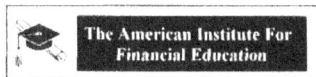 The American Institute
For Financial Education

4920 Roswell Road, Suite 45B-508
Atlanta, GA. 30342

Library of Congress Catalog Card Number: Applied

Howell, Jack D., Jr.
  Safeguarding Your Retirement:
  11 Key Steps to protect your retirement account / Jack D. Howell, Jr

  1. Investing. 2. Retirement Planning. 3. Asset Allocation

ISBN 0-9668050-2-X

"This publication is designed to provide accurate and authoritative information in regard to the subject matter covered. It is sold with the understanding that the publishers not engaged in rendering legal, accounting, or other professional service. If legal advice or expert assistance is required, the services of a professional person should be sought."
-From a Declaration of Principles jointly adopted by a Committee of the American Bar Association and a Committee of the Publishers and Associations.

Artwork by AIFE ………………………..   Atlanta, Georgia

Printed in the United States of America   1st Edition

Table Of Contents

Our Nation's retirement system is in a dramatic state of despair.

Most people are unaware of the massive shift that has taken place in how our country will provide for our future retirees. Because of this, we as a nation have many challenges and tough decisions ahead.

The Pension Plan

In the past, it was the responsibility of the **employer**, as well as the government, to provide income during the retirement years of our seniors. This was accomplished by the enactment of pension plans by corporations in partnership with the federal government, through granting special tax "incentives" to those corporations which enacted the government "approved" pension plans.

Because employees wanted security in the latter years of their lives, employers who possessed these plans enjoyed a competitive advantage when recruiting employees. The government, reasoned that giving corporations small tax advantages now for employee savings, would yield great benefits not only to employees, but also to society at large. So, it appeared as a "win, win, win" situation for all concerned.

1) The corporation would "win": by increasing their ability to attract more qualified employees because of the added benefits, also by having much of the cost for these added benefits born by the government through favorable tax treatment.

2) The employee would "win": by of the ever-increasing balance of their retirement account.

3) <u>The government would also "win"</u>: by having a senior population that was self-sustaining and therefore a benefit to overall economic activity, as opposed to a reliant and dependant senior population. The latter scenario would require the government to expend vast amounts of money to care for the senior population, which would inevitably slow or even depress overall economic activity.

For these reasons, the "Pension Plan" was born. It was designed to be the primary source of "non-governmental" retirement income for the nation's retirees.

Social Security

After the great depression and World War II the nation's population desired greater financial security. Although pension plans were already in place, they were only offered to a small portion of the workforce. A dynamic politician decided that all Americans should have the benefit of "pension plans," in effect, a pension plan for the common man, sponsored and maintained by the government. The name of the politician was Franklin Delano Roosevelt, and his revolutionary plan was termed: "The New Deal." From this "New Deal," what we know today as the system of "Social Security" was born. It appeared that the nation's seniors upon retirement would not only have all of their <u>basic</u> financial needs met, but would also be able to <u>enjoy</u> their leisure years. This plan worked well for America until the average age of the nation's populace began to change.

This shift in population arose when tens of thousand of soldiers and other military personnel, returned home to their wives and girlfriends after very long absences due to World War II.

As you might imagine, this reunion of loved ones led to a huge increase in the number of births in a relatively short period of time. As a matter of fact, these babies occurred in such large numbers they became know as those who were born during the "Baby Boom" period. And today, these people are commonly referred to as "Baby Boomers." However, this baby boom period is the primary cause of our current problem with social security.

When social security was first enacted as a federal program, there were approximately 12 workers paying into the system for every 1 retiree drawing money out of the system. However, today, as our nation's baby boomers move toward retirement, this 12 to 1 ratio continues to change dramatically. It is estimated that when baby boomers move into their retirement years (during the next 10-15 years) the social security ratio of "pay-ins" to "pay-outs" will diminish from the 12 to 1 that existed decades ago, to approximately 2 to 1. Yes, only 2 workers paying into the system for every 1 retiree drawing out of the system. It should be fairly easy to see the financial strains this ratio change brings, as well as the possibility of collapsing the entire social security system. We have all heard the politicians give their speeches,.. ranging from "the system is fine, no need to worry," to "the system will totally collapse and very soon." Reality probably lies somewhere between the two.

The 401K

The 401k and similar "self-retirement" saving plans, were initially an attempt to augment and supplement the already established corporate sponsored retirement plan, the pension plan, and the government sponsored retirement plan social security.

However, as 401k plans grew in popularity, corporations - in our opinion - allowed the 401k plan to "supplant and replace" the pension plan rather than to "augment and supplement" the pension plan.

The government, recognizing the inherent benefits of financially secure retiree's, encouraged corporations (through special tax breaks) to establish these types of "self-saving" retirement plans. These plans grew at mind-boggling rates, both in number and asset size. Everything looked fine. American workers now had three financial plans specifically designed to provide for their retirement years.
1) Pension Plans
2) Social Security
3) 401k Plans

Politicians felt, with good reason, that they had provided all the tools, maybe even more than needed, for the American worker to retire financially secure. But, something went wrong on America's road to a financially secure retirement. What went wrong created a "New Reality."

The New Reality

The New Reality is Pension Plans cover fewer and fewer people. The reason: with pension plans, the corporation is responsible for providing for the workers financial retirement security. In our opinion, corporations decided it would be in their best interest not to shoulder this "long-term" financial commitment due to the obvious and enormous liability that was attached to such a commitment. As the 401-K increased in popularity, corporations offered fewer pension plans, and more and more 401k plans. In fact, most Americans are now covered by 401k plans rather than pension plans.

At the same time, politicians have been continuously taking money out of the social security trust fund and using it for their "general operating budget" purposes, further eroding our government's ability to meet its social security obligation. The extent of this erosion is so vast that many feel our government will default on its social security promise. In fact, social security **WILL** be changed, what remains to be decided is the scope and extent of the changes.

What began as a three-pronged approach to secure the financial retirement of the American worker has evolved into a single approach: - The 401k or Individual approach.

Herein lies the "New Reality," in fact, a "New Responsibility," one that Americans have not been responsible for in many decades.

The New Reality: providing for your own financial retirement security.

Let us say this once more:

Pension Plans are not available to most American workers, in fact they never were truly available to all. Social security benefits are at best unknown, therefore, if you are to live your senior years in comfort with financial security,... **YOU MUST provide for yourself.**

This is a fundamental change in our retirement system and the effects of which will be undoubtedly analyzed, studied, and written about for many generations to come.

This publication attempts to convey to the reader what we feel are the 11 most important factors to achieve and maintain financial security for your retirement . Regardless of the readers age or income, we believe following these guidelines will substantially increase your knowledge and thereby increase your ability to obtain your financial goals and live your retirement life with security, comfort, and dignity.

KEY STEP #1

DIVERSIFICATION

Diversification has long been acknowledged as a prudent rule of human behavior. This rule supersedes financial investments and indeed permeates all of society. An example would be the old saying, "don't put all of your eggs in one basket," In this saying the "basket" would be akin to an asset class.

Any particular event, financial or otherwise (such as a terrorist attack), could impact one particular segment of the financial markets at any time. If you are only invested in the segment impacted by the "bad news," the value of your investments could decline substantially. However, if your investments are **truly** diversified, the negative impact of any one event on your overall portfolio will be greatly reduced. Why? The odds are considerably smaller that some single event would cause all investment to suffer a similar decline in value.

This principle was very dramatically demonstrated during the terrorist attack of September 11, 2001. While this one single event caused every sector to decline very sharply, most sectors recovered in a relatively short period of time. However, one sector, such as airlines, have remained depressed long after the initial shock. If your portfolio was truly diversified it would have regained most of its value in a relatively short period of time. If your investment portfolio was not truly diversified, such as being heavily invested in the airline or transportation sector only, there would be much greater uncertainty with regard to the likelihood of a portfolio rebound and the length of time necessary to achieve the rebound.

The key is **"TRUE"** diversification. On many occasions investors believe they are diversified because they have

various types of mutual funds in their retirement account, but often, these same investors are not aware of the types of funds actually in their retirement plan. So, while they may have four different funds, all four may be of the same asset class. For instance, all investment in "high growth" stock funds, or all in "safety" funds such as various bond funds. This represents what we call "intra" class diversification, and while intra-class diversification is preferable to no diversification, it is NOT TRUE DIVERSIFICATION.

In order to achieve the safety afforded by diversification, investors must actually achieve "TRUE" diversification.

True diversification means diversification "<u>across</u>" asset classes, not merely "<u>within</u>" asset classes.

For example, if your portfolio is divided into 10 large company stocks, you are diversified "within" an asset class. The class being large company stocks. If your portfolio is spread across bonds of 10 different companies, again, you are diversified "within" the bond asset class. To achieve "true" diversification the investor must diversify **<u>among and between</u>** asset classes.

The primary asset classes are listed below:

A.) Large Domestic Stocks
B.) Small Domestic Stocks
C.) Bonds
D.) Cash Equivalents (CD's, Money Markets)
E.) International Stocks
F.) Precious Metals

Asset class yields vary during different economic climates. The investor will benefit greatly by having a general understanding of the asset classes listed above and their corresponding "historical-yield" during various economic climates.

KEY STEP #2

ASSET ALLOCATION

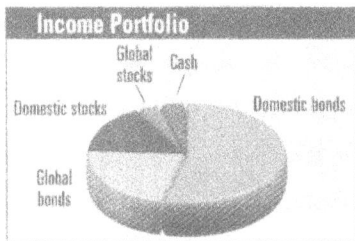

Income Portfolio
Global stocks
Cash
Domestic stocks
Domestic bonds
Global bonds
Source: Mark M. Spradley, Paine Webber

Asset allocation is certainly one of the most, if not **the most**, important criteria in the investing process. Asset allocation, when used properly, can help an investor match the amount of risk and return of the portfolio with the "stage of life" of the investor. In addition, the investor can utilize the principles of asset allocation to reduce their risk exposure to any particular asset class when deemed necessary. The principle of asset allocation was developed from analysis of past asset class performance over multi-decade periods. This analysis revealed much information, the most important of which is detailed below.

- First, we learned that certain asset classes have greater "average" yields. While some asset classes averaged nearly 10% per year, others averaged as low as 3% per year.
- Second, we learned that asset classes have varying volatility. In other words, the asset classes that yielded 10%, also sometimes lost a substantial portion of their value, and asset classes that returned smaller yields, had a much smaller percent of loss in any given year.
- Third, we learned that not all asset classes move "up" at the same time. For example, stocks tend to perform better during an economic climate of prosperity, while bonds typically perform better during times of economic decline. Equipped with this information investors can make portfolio "allocation" shifts in accordance with their assessment of current and future economic activity.

These 3 facts form the foundation of asset allocation principles.

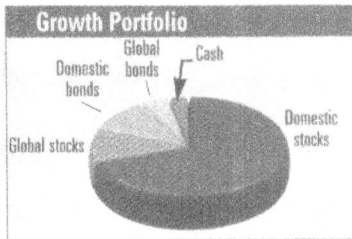

Growth Portfolio

For example, a few relevant factors are listed below:

- The risk tolerance of the individual.
- The individual's overall financial situation.
- Years to desired retirement.
- The individuals perception of the current overall economy and it's "near-to-intermediate" term future.

Of course, these factors will vary according to the individual, that is precisely why it is difficult to prepare a "one plan fits all" investment plan. It is extremely important for the individual to assess the factors above and if necessary discuss them with a financial planner for further clarification and understanding. Remember, proper asset allocation is thought by some to account for as much as 80-90% of a portfolio's yield performance. The key to proper asset allocation, is having proper **balance**.

KEY STEP #3

RE-BALANCE - BEFORE RETIRE

As stated previously, your needs will not be the same at 60 years old as they are at 20. Similarly, your needs at 50 will not be the same as they are at 40, or 30. This means as you move through life and your needs and financial situation changes, the asset allocation of your retirement funds must also change. Changes you make in your asset allocation are referred to as **re-balancing**.

Re-balancing is **crucial** to your financial retirement security. We cannot stress this strongly enough. To ignore **re-balancing** your financial retirement assets could expose you to catastrophic financial loss, eliminating the possibility of a comfortable senior retirement.

Re-balancing is not a science, rather think of it more as an art form. Only the investor, maybe in consultation with family or other advisors, can address the factors listed above and balance their asset class mix in a manner that affords opportunity, security, and comfort. However, there are several models which have been developed to serve as a guide. A few of these models are listed below, but I must stress once more, these are only guides and the individual should seek the advice and counsel of professionals to ensure their specific asset allocation mix is appropriate for their goals and objectives, both long and short term.

SAMPLE ASSET ALLOCATION MODELS

Example 1

Years to Retirement: 20 or more

Profile: Investor who believes stocks offer superior
returns, desires a 10% annual return

Based on an expected return of 10.0%, this is your suggested portfolio mix.

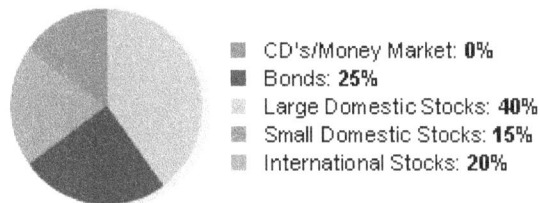

- CD's/Money Market: **0%**
- Bonds: **25%**
- Large Domestic Stocks: **40%**
- Small Domestic Stocks: **15%**
- International Stocks: **20%**

RISK
The annual risk associated with a return of 10% is **high**.

Example 2

Years to Retirement: 5 - 10

Profile: Your 401k likely to be your total nest egg, you
desire less risk with opportunity for growth.

Based on an expected return of 8.0%, this is your suggested portfolio mix.

- CD's/Money Market: **20%**
- Bonds: **50%**
- Large Domestic Stocks: **15%**
- Small Domestic Stocks: **5%**
- International Stocks: **10%**

RISK
The annual risk associated with a return of 8% is **moderate**.

Example 3

Years to Retirement: 5 or less

Profile: Your 401k is likely to be your total nest egg,
other than social security

Based on an expected return of 6.5%, this is your suggested portfolio mix.

- CD's/Money Market: **50%**
- Bonds: **30%**
- Large Domestic Stocks: **10%**
- Small Domestic Stocks: **5%**
- International Stocks: **5%**

RISK
The Annual risk associated with a return of 6.5% is **low to moderate**.

Example 4

Years to Retirement: Already Retired

Profile: Living off 401k saving, social security,
and other personal savings.

Based on an expected return of 5.0%, this is your suggested portfolio mix.

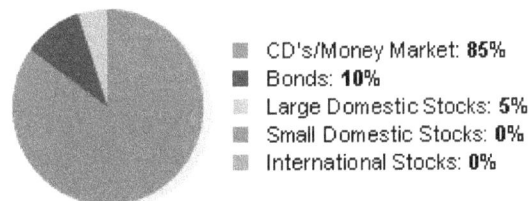

- CD's/Money Market: **85%**
- Bonds: **10%**
- Large Domestic Stocks: **5%**
- Small Domestic Stocks: **0%**
- International Stocks: **0%**

RISK
The Annual risk associated with a return of 5% is **very low**.

One final point, the "sample" asset allocation models shown above are for **illustrative** purposes only, investors should develop models based on their individual goals, objectives, and financial situation. Seek advice if necessary.

KEY STEP #4

MAXIMIZE YOUR CONTRIBUTIONS

Saving is not very easy for most of the American population. As a matter of fact, Americans are about the worst savers in the world when compared with other industrialized nations. The reason is because we have been conditioned to spend, in essence a *live for the day* frame of mind. While this gives us short-term gratification, it steadily and continually erodes the security of our financial future.

Government has played a role also. Our federal government has continually encouraged our citizens to spend, rather than save. The rationale is that spending increases economic activity, which spurs job growth, productivity, and helps to keep the economy out of recession. This is not necessarily a flawed strategy, except when an economic downturn inevitably occurs, the American populous, in general, is much worse off because they lack an "emergency" fund or adequate savings to sustain themselves during the period of economic decline. In addition, our government has mostly believed that corporate pensions and social security would be sufficient to take care of our senior population. Recently, however, we have seen a dramatic shift in this thinking.

It appears our government has finally realized that the ever-dwindling number of corporate pensions coupled with increased *insecurity* of social security, necessitates increased levels of individual savings if our future senior population is to live in dignity and with financial security.

This newly formed realization by our government is extremely important for every American worker. Why? The government, recognizing that social security and pensions will not be sufficient, is for the first time in this country's history, not only allowing but actively encouraging increased individual savings.

It is doing so by phasing in higher and higher 401k and IRA contribution limits over the next few years. The phase in limits are listed below.

Annual 401k Contribution Limits

Year	Regular	Over age 50
2001	$10,500	$10,500
2002	11,000	12,000
2003	12,000	14,000
2004	13,000	16,000
2005	14,000	18,000
2006	15,000	20,000

Annual IRA Contribution Limits

Year	Regular	Over age 50
2001	$2,000	$2,000
2002	3,000	3,500
2003	3,000	3,500
2004	3,000	3,500
2005	4,000	4,500
2006	4,000	5,000
2007	4,000	5,000
2008	5,000	6,000

It is **imperative** that individuals take advantage of these increased limits and contribute the maximum. The retirement balance difference, irrespective of salary, between a contribution of 3%, 5%, 10%, and 15%, over a 10, 20, or 30 year period is staggering. Workers should not base their contributions on their employers matching policy, but rather they should view their contributions as securing their retirement. Any amount the employer contributes is just extra.

For many decades the government was not assertive nor did they provide the proper tools to help spur individual savings rates; now they finally have and the American workers MUST do **whatever is necessary** to maximize retirement contributions and take full advantage of this opportunity to secure the financial future of themselves and their families.

Maximizing Your Money

KEY STEP #5

MONITOR MONTHLY / QUARTERLY RETURNS

Far too many people do not look at the monthly or quarterly statements provided to them by the company which handles their retirement funds. We cannot possibly relate to you how many of our associates have asked us questions about their retirement allocation, and in return, we ask them what are they invested in currently. Invariably, the answer we receive is, "I don't know". Our second question, "what was your percentage return last year or last quarter?" Again the answer is, "I don't know". Individuals must have an awareness of their investments the yield performance of those investments.

The point is this: the American worker MUST:

1) **Understand the types of investments he or she has in their retirement plan.**
2) **Know the specific stocks, bonds or mutual funds in their retirement plan**
3) **Understand what the average returns are for their specific investment type**
4) **Know what the specific returns are for your specific investments**

At the very least, individuals should understand and know the information listed above. This information is not very difficult to obtain and once this monitoring has begun, will take very little time or effort, maybe as little as a few minutes per week. And for those workers with a computer in their home a few minutes per month.

20

One last point, if your retirement fund is yielding 5%, that might be above or on par with other funds in your particular asset group. However, it might also be drastically lower. If you do not have any idea of what is <u>typical</u> for your <u>type</u> of investment, you cannot judge the performance of your retirement fund. Therefore, as stated above and here more succinctly, the individual must know what they have, how it is performing, and how that performance compares to similar investment types.

Monitor the performance of your retirement account(s) and make adjustments when and where necessary.

Stop Profit ---- Stop Loss

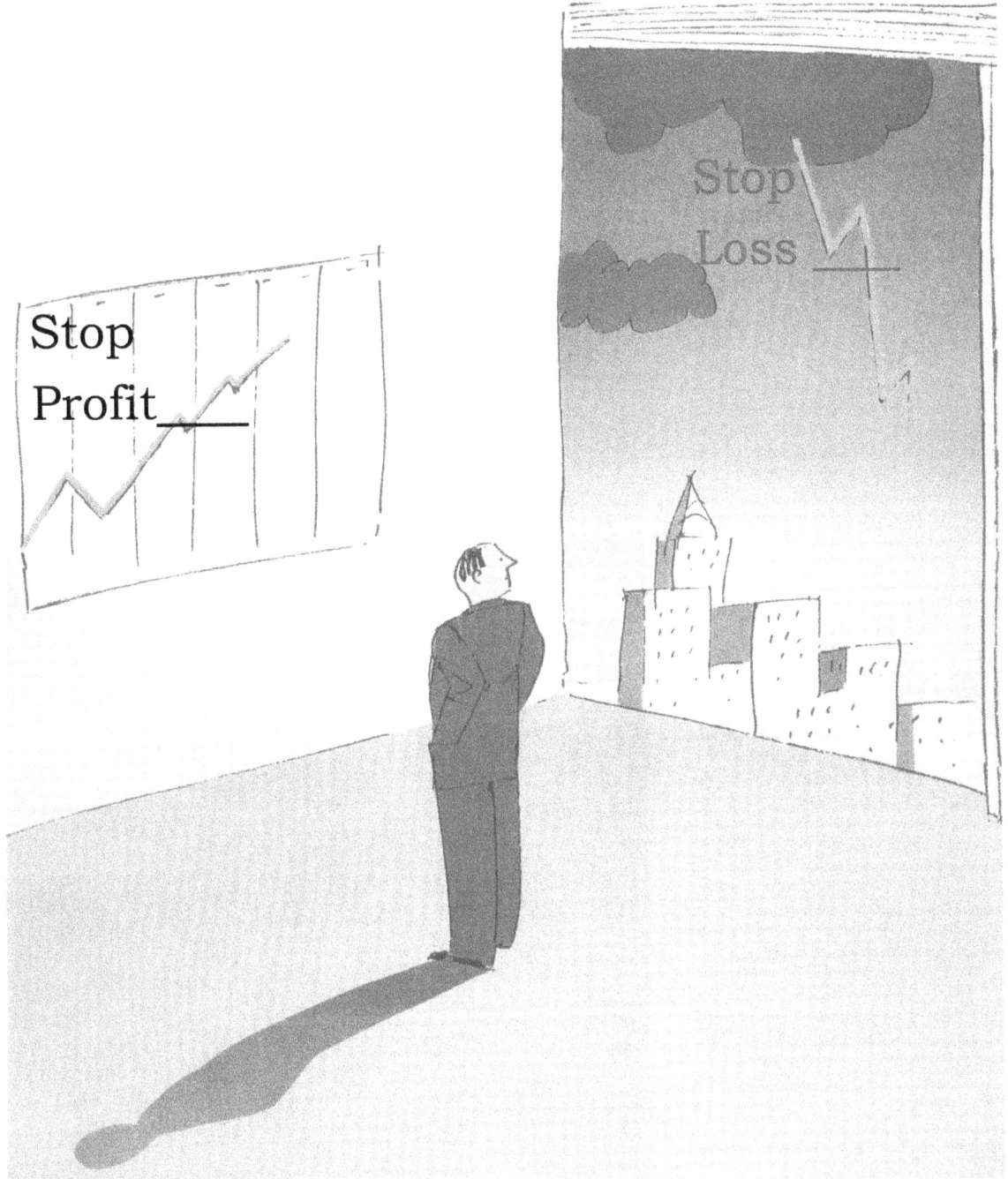

KEY STEP # 6

HAVE A "STOP LOSS" AND "STOP PROFIT" STRATEGY

The Stop-Loss

This will save you from quickly losing your entire retirement nest egg. For far TOO long the "professionals" have been advising the public to hold onto your investments "no matter what." They constantly say, "you're in for the long-run." Well, one statement said "in the long-run, we're all dead." So, we are not really investing for the long-run, but rather we are investing for a specific period of time, in order to meet a specific set of goals. Armed with this new perspective, we can now start to "manage" our investments a little better.

Sometimes in life, we make mistakes. These mistakes occur in every facet of our life. They sometimes occur at work, sometimes while we are driving, sometimes when we are ordering from a menu, and sometimes when we decide what movie to go see. These mistakes generally cause us very little financial loss and mostly result in just a minor inconvenience. However, mistakes in the financial markets can be disastrous. Obviously, if we as human beings make mistakes in almost every other facet of life, it stands to reason that we might *choose* the wrong stock, bond, or mutual fund, or just happen to invest at the wrong time (such as when the entire market is in a downtrend). In order to protect the bulk of your retirement assets, the individual MUST have what is referred to in the brokerage industry as a **"stop-loss"** point.

The stop-loss is designed to do exactly what its name implies; to stop your financial losses. For example, if an investor purchased a mutual fund (or stock) at $25.00 per share, and decided that he or she would only tolerate a mistake (or loss) of 10%, the stop loss point would be $22.50. A different investor might decide to allow the investment to decline by 20% before considering that investment a "mistake." In that scenario, the mutual fund (or stock) could decline in price to $20.00. In either case, the investor would sell the investment immediately after the price matched or fell below the pre-determined stop loss price. This is one of the most valued and important rules which professional money managers utilize.

Everyone should have and adhere to their stop loss prices. **The key is to determine the maximum loss you are willing to sustain "prior" to purchasing the investment and then obey your price limits.** Why? **After** the purchase your psychology changes and you are less objective about what you will consider a mistake. Therefore always decide at what price you will consider the investment a "mistake" prior to the purchase, and remain disciplined enough to take the appropriate action.

If you made a mistake by ordering an entrée you did not like, would you continue to eat the entrée? Of course not, you would order another selection or even go to another restaurant; the fact that you ordered something that did not meet your expectations is *acceptable*, it happens in life, you just move on to another selection. The investor must be able to consider his or her investments in the same light. It is also *acceptable* to make an "investment mistake," just stop your losses, peruse the "investment menu" once again and make another selection.

This one simple rule, if obeyed, will save your retirement account an untold amount of money over the span of your working and retirement years. This rule, if followed, will prevent your retirement account from losing a catastrophic amount in any one investment. **Remember one of the most important keys to making money is to learn how to avoid losing it.**

The Stop-Profit

Well, this is peculiar, why would anyone want to **stop** his or her profit? The reason you have a "stop-profit" price limit is simple.

1) Nothing goes up forever
2) Things come down quicker than they go up (it's nature)
3) Statistics and Probabilities are important

1) Nothing goes up forever:

Most people will agree with this statement. Applying this statement to investments which have gone up in price since they were purchased, leaves one only question remaining: "when will the price of the investment go down".

Obviously, no one knows when the investment will decline in price, therefore, the individual worker/investor must decide how much of their "**profit**" he or she is willing to "forfeit" before liquidating the investment. If the answer is "none," the individual would sell immediately, however, that eliminates the possibility of even greater gains.

Lets revisit our previous example where the investor purchased the mutual fund (or stock) at $25.00 dollars. Assume one year has passed and the mutual fund is now priced at $35.00. The investor has a profit of $10.00 in this investment, how much should he or she be willing to lose before selling?

If the investor decided to risk 10% of his/her profit they would have - what I have termed - a "**stop- profit**" sell price of $34.00 (10% of $10.00 profit). If another investor is willing to risk 50% of his/her profit, then a price limit of $30.00 would be set as the "**stop-profit**" point. Where you set your stop-profit will depend on many individual factors, but what is **most important** is that you recognize that *nothing goes up* forever, and you should be prepared to liquidate when you reach your "stop-profit" price.

2) Things come down quicker than they go up (it's nature):

If you have any experience with the financial markets, you understand this statement to be true. If you do not have experience with the financial markets, you will recognize this statement to be true in the not too distant future. Hopefully, if you follow the guidelines in this guide, you will not have to learn firsthand.

Things do come down quicker than they go up. Ever seen a balloon go up, then come down? Financial assets react in a very similar fashion. Why? Because selling is usually sparked by some event which leads to the masses all trying to "get out" at the same time. This "mad dash for the door" often leads to very quick and dramatic declines in financial asset prices. Again, another reason to have your "stop-profit" price limit already determined.

3) Statistics and Probabilities are important:

This statement focuses on the absolute necessity for investment education. Picking your stop-profit price limits is much easier if you have an idea of how much certain assets appreciate, on average, during the course of one year.

For instance, investors should know that large company stocks usually return about 10% per year.

Equipped with this knowledge, if the large company stock in your portfolio has appreciated 30% in price within the last year, you would know that you now have a return equal to "three years" the normal return for large company stocks. What should you do? Well, no one can answer that question but you, however, you are now forming your answer based on knowledge and awareness.

Again, with a 30% return in one year you now have a 200% higher return than what is normal. Put in this perspective, you might not decide to sell, but you would certainly be much more cautious because, 1) statistically your return is abnormal; and 2) probabilities suggest that a more normal return is likely. The only way a "more normal" return can materialize is for your stock price to decline. Let me state emphatically, this does not mean the price will not continue to rise, it very well might, however every dollar increase in price should make you more and more cautious about the investment.

At some point in time you have to consider the first statement in this section; "Nothing goes up forever." If you set your stop-profit price as a percent of profit you will notice as the stocks' price increases, your stop-profit price also increases. This is appropriate, just remember, when the price starts to decline and eventually reaches your stop-profit price, be disciplined, adhere to your stop-profit price and liquidate.

Do not focus on how much you "could have made" if you had not sold, rather stay focused on how much you did make and how much less risk you are now holding. **Remember your goal: "to have a financially secure retirement", not to "get rich quick" in the stock market.** "Greed will eventually lead to ruin."

KEY STEP #7

ROLLOVER NOT ROLLOUT

Decades ago, the American worker would generally stay with one or two employers for the duration of their career. However, times have changed. Today's American worker changes jobs, on average, 5-7 times during a lifetime of working. How you manage your retirement funds during these job changes will severely impact your retirement life.

When you change jobs, most 401k plans offer you the opportunity to take your "cash" out of the plan. If you do so, you can either take the money and move it into another "tax qualified" plan, or just take the cash and use it as an unexpected windfall. The first scenario is called a "Rollover," the second scenario I have termed a "Rollout."

While most of us could use the extra cash from a "rollout," the individual MUST resist this temptation, because if you "rollout," you are in essence "starting over" in your financial retirement life. This practice would be unthinkable in your professional career. Imagine if every time you changed jobs, you would accept an offer to start at the bottom and work your way back up. Then after a few more years with the new company, you receive an offer which gives you lower pay, fewer benefits, less autonomy, and less responsibility. Again, navigating your professional career in this manner would be unthinkable. However, that is precisely what you do in your "financial retirement career" if you "rollout". If you "rollover" you continue to move yourself up the ladder of financial retirement security.

There are tax consequences depending on which decision you make. If you **rollover** (into an IRA or other "tax qualified" plan), the government allows you to do so without any tax bill or penalty. Conversely, if you **rollout**, there are huge negative tax implications. First, you must account for the distribution as "ordinary income" and pay all the "regular" taxes due on the lump sum AND pay a 10% "penalty" tax as well.

The government recognizes the benefit to the individual and the future benefit to society in choosing the rollover option, therefore, through tax policy, the government attempts to persuade you to make the right choice. The "rollover" just happens to be one decision that is in the best interest of all parties involved, best for the individual, the individual's family, society at large, and the government.

Once again, when changing jobs never "start over" in your financial retirement life by choosing to "rollout". Always, always, always… continue moving toward your goal of financial security by choosing to "rollover".

KEY STEP #8

DOLLAR COST AVERAGE

This principle sounds scientific but it's actually very simple. This principle put in other words simply means always continue to invest. To some this may sound scary but it is much safer to invest your funds over a long period of time as opposed to buying in one lump sum. To illustrate further, let's look at a simple example.

Suppose you had $24, 000.00 to invest during 2001 and you decided to invest all $24,000.00 in Cisco Systems. Below are two analyses. First, is the result of investing all $24,000.00 in the first week of January 2001; and second, the results of investing the $24,000.00 in 12 equal installments of $2,000.00 on the 1st week of every month.

Analysis 1   Lump Sum Investment

Invest $24,000 "Lump Sum" in Cisco Systems as of January 5, 2001

Price of Cisco = $36.63   No. of Shares = 655
Value of Investment = $24,000.00

*As of January 4, 2002

  Price of Cisco = $20.83   No. of Shares = 655

Value of Investment = $13,643.65
                                    43% Loss

<u>Analysis 2</u>   <u>Dollar Cost Average Over Time</u>

Invest $24,000 in "Equal Installments" of $2000.00
Per Month in Cisco Systems over 12 month period

Start date: January 5, 2001

<u>Date</u>	<u>Amount</u>	<u>Price</u>	<u>No. of Shares Purchased</u>
1/5/01	2000.00	36.63	55
2/2/01	2000.00	35.50	56
3/2/01	2000.00	22.19	90
4/6/01	2000.00	13.63	147
5/4/01	2000.00	19.64	102
6/1/01	2000.00	18.85	106
7/6/01	2000.00	16.79	119
8/3/01	2000.00	20.05	100
9/7/01	2000.00	14.36	139
10/5/01	2000.00	14.94	134
11/2/01	2000.00	17.26	116
12/7/01	2000.00	21.16	95
Total	24,000.00		1259

Closing Price January 4, 2002 = $20.83
Total Shares Purchased =   1259

Value of Investment as of January 4, 2002 = $26,224.97
Average Cost per share ………………   = $19.06

By employing a "Dollar Cost average" approach, the per
share average cost was lowered by 48%. Also, the investor
realized an investment gain of $2,224.97.

Most dramatic is the net value of the investment:
        Analysis 1 = Lump Sum   = $13,643.65
        Analysis 2 = Dollar Cost Avg. = $26,224.97

Dollar Cost Average method **Doubled** Lump Sum Method

As you can see, investing the funds over time generated a greater return. This may not be the result on every occasion and the potential for greater return is not the primary reason to "dollar cost average." Investing in equal installments works to the benefit of the individual over time primarily because as the stock (or mutual fund) price increases, the investor purchases fewer shares. Conversely, as the stock price decreases, the investor purchases more share, and over time, the investor is accumulating more shares at lower prices, fewer shares at higher prices, which ultimately lowers the average "cost" of the investment.

Obviously, the lower the average cost, the higher the potential gain. Again, as stated in a previous section of this publication, most of us cannot predict with any degree of accuracy when a stock price will go up or down; however, we do know with absolute certainty that prices will fluctuate. Therefore, utilizing a "dollar cost average" strategy will, over time, enable the investor to realize an overall lower average price per share. **When at all possible,….. Dollar Cost Average.**

KEY STEP #9

BE CAUTIOUS OF EMPLOYER STOCK

The most infamous example of catastrophic loss related to employer stock is that of Enron Corporation. Many of its employees lost their entire life savings all within a few months. Former Enron employees have told their stories on national television news programs, and testified in numerous congressional hearings. For those who are unaware of Enron, it is a company whose stock price hit a high of around 80 in early 2001, and collapsed to just pennies by the end of the year. The stock price lost over 99% of its value all in a few months. That means employees who had their retirement fund balance invested solely in Enron stock lost over 99% of their retirement fund. Put in more visual terms, an employee with Enron stock in their retirement plan worth $200,000 at the high, had an account value of less than $2,000.00 in just a few short months. The number of employees with similar stories is just horrific.

It would be a grave mistake to believe this was a "one time only" phenomenon, if fact, there are many large companies whose stock prices have lost **80-90% of their value** (between High and Low price) during the period January 1, 2000 and December 31, 2001. Many of these are Fortune 500 companies whose employees felt safe and secure with their employers stock in their retirement plan. For those employees with less than 10 years to retirement, their financial security has been shattered. Even those with 20 or more years to retirement have endured a catastrophic financial blow. Let us stress again, the number of companies and the names of these companies are so surprising it would shock most American workers and politicians. Listed below are just a few of the companies who fall into this category.

January 1, 2000 - December 31, 2001

Company	High	Low	% Difference
Halliburton	$55.18	8.60	84% loss
Motorola	61.54	10.50	83% loss
Enron	90.75	.56	99% loss
Lucent	77.50	6.00	92% loss
Sun Micro.	64.65	7.78	88% loss
Schwab	44.75	8.13	82% loss
Juniper Net.	244.50	8.90	96% loss
Cienna	151.00	9.20	94% loss
Corning	113.33	7.52	93% loss

The most important lesson in this section relates to our previous section on diversification. Never should the individual have the bulk of their retirement funds in any one asset class, **including company stock**. **Always diversify across asset classes and types.**

Please understand, investing in your employers stock is not always a dangerous or risky decision. Obviously, if your employer will only make "matching contributions" to your 401k with company stock, it would be in your best interest to accept the contribution. The **mistake**, however, would be to take "**your contribution**" and further invest in your employers stock. If you do not have the option of diversifying with your "employer match" contribution, then by all means diversify with "your contribution" dollars.

Regretfully, this publication was not available prior to the Enron situation; many of the "11 key steps" presented herein could have prevented the demise of many Enron employee retirement accounts. Please be aware, there are many other Enron type disasters looming, and hopefully this publication will help **you** protect **your** retirement fund from similar catastrophic losses.

KEY STEP #10

LIVE BELOW YOUR MEANS,
SAVE AND INVEST THE REST

While this "key" is simple to understand, it is incredibly difficult to implement. As Americans, we are accustomed to buying whatever we want, whenever we want it. If we cannot pay with cash, we simply use credit. Whether we use cash or credit, we generally refuse to do "without" for any sustained period of time. You, the reader, must change this ideology.

Most of us, if we tried, could easily reduce our housing payment by $100.00 or $200.00 per month. We could also drive a less expensive car and save an additional $100.00 per month. We could "entertain" ourselves a little less (not much), and save another $100.00 per month. That would be an additional $400.00 a month or $4,800.00 a year in savings. If the individual invested that savings over 20 to 30 years, the accumulated earnings is staggering. Again, for a more visual understanding, a few examples with varying interest rates are shown below.

Monthly Savings	# of Years	Rate of Int.	Balance
$200	10	5 %	$31,186
200	10	8	36,833
200	10	10	41,310
400	10	5	62,371
400	10	8	73,666
400	10	10	82,620

Monthly Savings	# of Years	Rate of Int.	Balance
$200	20	5 %	$ 82,549
200	20	8	118,589
200	20	10	153,139
400	20	5	165,098
400	20	8	237,179
400	20	10	306,278

Living below your means does not equate to lowering your living standard or depriving yourself or your family of the necessities for a safe and comfortable life; rather, it just requires you to "shave" a little off around the "edges." With a little forethought and planning, most of us can easily save $200-$400 without really even noticing it. If you invest this savings wisely, it could very well be the difference between a retirement of comfort or worry.

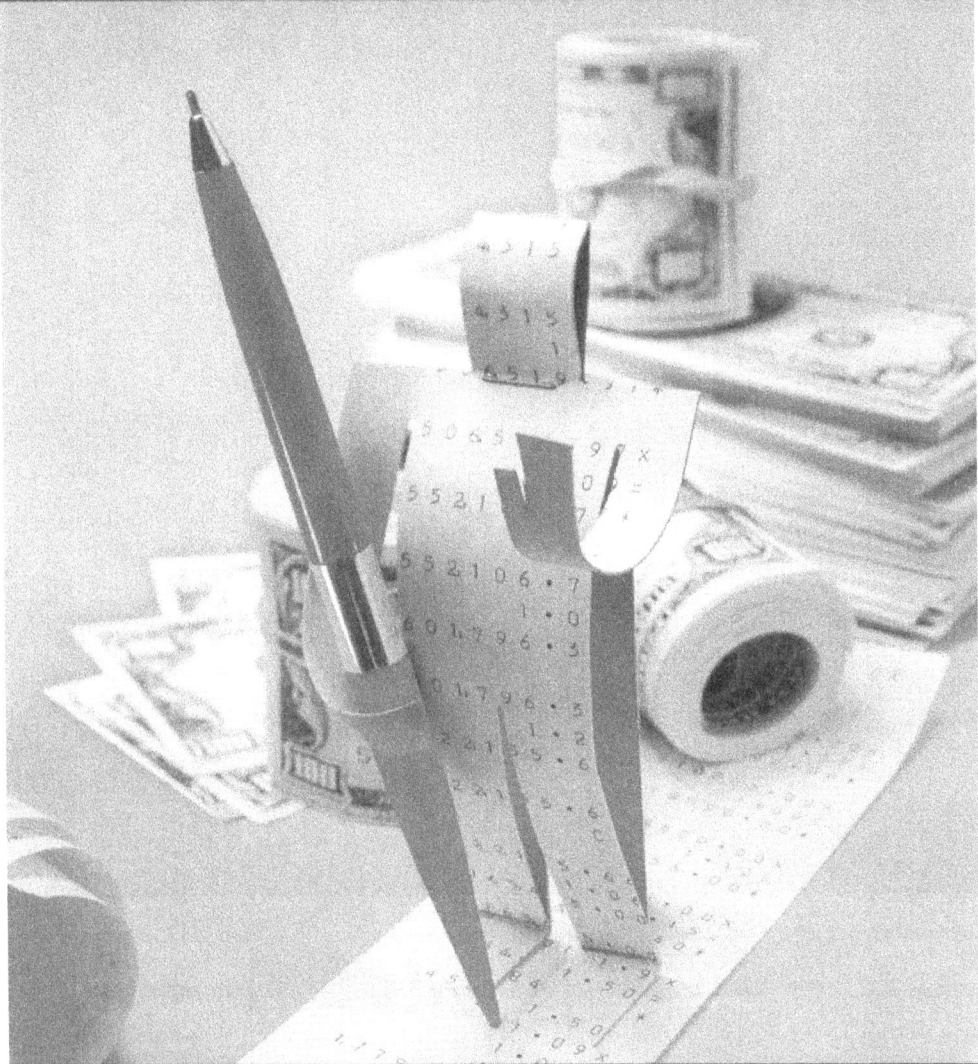

KEEPING IT

REQUIRES

KNOWLEDGE

KEY STEP #11

EDUCATION, EDUCATION, EDUCATION

In the previous pages, many principles of wealth creation and preservation have been covered, however, all of these principles are based on the premise of, and work better with, **increased investment education**.

Other than one's individual health, a person's financial knowledge is probably the most significant factor in determining the "**quality of life**" for that person and their family. Yet and still, most American workers assign a very low priority and place very little importance, on investment education. There are several reasons for this "lack of enthusiasm" about investment education.

1) Investment Education is Difficult

Many decades ago, the stock market was looked upon as something only the rich could access. It was different from most other types of public "buying" and "selling." Typically an individual would walk into a retail establishment, make a selection, and then pay for the item. With stock purchases it was different.

First, you could not "see" the items, second, the prices were obscured in fractions, and third, you could not make the purchase yourself; someone else called a "stockbroker" purchased it for you. Through all of this, the public gained a "sense" that stock purchasing MUST be difficult due to the complexities of purchasing and the peculiar way in which the prices were reflected. Generations of Americans never tried to educate themselves about investing because of this *perceived* difficulty. And as any psychologist or sociologist will attest, perception is reality.

2) <u>Investing Is Risky</u>

Most Americans also have the perception that the stock market is extremely risky. This perception, in large part, was born from the stock market crash of 1929. While there have been other sharp stock market declines, the decline of 1929 was much more injurious to investor perception due to the overall economic state during that same time, which just happened to be this nation's only "depression" in modern time. The stock market decline of 1987 was so very quickly reversed that the psychological effect was much less damaging. The latest major decline (NASDAQ 2000-2001) has already been somewhat prolonged. If it continues, this "risk perception" will likely escalate once again, maybe even reaching levels not seen since the early 1930's.

2) <u>How and Where To Learn</u>

Investment education has not been readily available to the masses. In general, the only methods of educating oneself about investments were from a family member who had the required knowledge, or a graduate school course. Until recently, most undergraduate studies programs did not offer investment education courses, and many still do not.

All of these factors have contributed to keeping the American worker somewhat afraid of investment education. However, the investment world has changed, ... dramatically.

Stock prices are now shown in dollars and cents as other products. This change was made for the expressed purpose of making it *easier* for every American to participate in the financial markets. Also, with the introduction of the internet, individuals can, if they choose, purchase investments themselves without the assistance of others.

These changes have led to massive numbers of Americans venturing into the stock market as "first generation" investors. These "first generation" investors, however, are not equipped with the required knowledge to navigate successfully through investing minefields. These investors are destined to lose vast amounts of money as they gain their investment education through the "school of hard knocks." When the stock market teaches investment education lessons, it generally charges a very high "tuition" for those lessons.

<u>Investment education is the key to a financially stable life, and secure retirement.</u> You are beginning your journey by reading, understanding, and implementing the keys explained in this booklet. However, your investment education should not stop with this booklet. This booklet is the "starting" line, you should continue to read and familiarize yourself with tools that provide **true** investment education. True investment education does not seek to give you advice, nor does it attempt to persuade you with whom to invest; but rather, true investment education merely seeks to provide the individual with the required unbiased information needed to make your own investment decision.

With fundamental investment education, even if you choose to consult with other investment professionals, you will do so in a much more informed manner and be able to recognize whether or not the professional is adequately serving your investment interests. Without a basic understanding of investments, a financial advisor or planner could lead you in any path he or she chooses and you would not have the ability to ascertain whether that path was leading to the achievement of your long term retirement goals.

Therefore, we urge you to take your time and re-read this material. Discuss it with others if you choose, but most importantly, take action and implement the knowledge you have gained by reading this book. Lastly, continue to improve your investment education knowledge. The more you know, the more you will have at retirement.

Remember,... no one cares more about YOUR money than you.

Educate yourself then take advantage of your knowledge!!

Additional Investment Education Resourcess

The American Institute For Financial Education published this book to inform the American public of certain "keys steps" to take to help protect their financial retirement fund. We strongly urge the individual to continue the investment education process through one of our other products listed below.

1) **Fundamentals of Investments in U.S. Financial Markets,**
   This is 254 page Hard/Soft cover book which covers all aspects of Individual Investing. Chapters include: Stocks, Bonds, Mutual Funds, Research, and an in-depth chapter of how the stock market actually works. $29.95

2) **Fundamentals of Investments in U.S. Financial Markets, Study Guide**
   Softcover: Has questions for every chapter of the hardcover book to aid the Individual in their study process. Also, each answer is given with a complete explanation of the logic and rationale. $24.95

3) **Safe-Guarding Your Retirement**
   Softcover: A 50 page guide detailing "11 Key Steps" to take to protect your retirement account. $24.95

4) **Invest Smarter, Profit More - Seminar**
   Video of actual investment seminar taught using

   Fundamentals of Investment in U.S. Financial Markets, as the course textbook. Watch and listen as the instructor covers "step-by-step" the book's subject matter. Also learn by hearing actual seminar participants as they ask questions and receive detailed explanations. (Run time approx. 6 hours.)

   USB Drive, (1 Drive) $39.99   CD Package, (11 CD's) $39.99
   DVD Package, (2 DVD's) $39.99

5) Internet Access Password

Allows access to the "members only" portion of our website. Provides a "my tutor" question link. Ask any question you may have here, guaranteed to be answered within 24 - 48hrs., (now you have your own personal tutor as you learn) Also updates on retirement information, informative news articles, continuing education resources, and access to special promotions.

Quarterly Subscription $39.99   Annual Subscription 79.99

6) Our All Inclusive Package

"Invest Smarter,…. Profit More"
Investment Education Course

BEST VALUE!!   Includes all Items listed below.

1) Fundamentals of Investments in U.S. Financial Markets - Textbook
2) Fundamentals of Investments in U.S. Financial Markets, Study Guide
3) Safe-Guarding Your Retirement - Textbook
4) Invest Smarter, Profit More - USB Video Seminar Set
5) Invest Smarter, Profit More - CD Seminar Set
6) Invest Smarter, Profit More - DVD Seminar Set
7) Internet Access Password   - Annual Subscription
8) Discount Coupon - 20% off Live or Virtual Seminars

A complete and comprehensive investment education package………. $99.99 ($399 value purchased separately)

Includes USB, DVD and CD video package, as well as **annual internet access password.

7) Register for our **"Live"**

"Invest Smarter,... Profit More"

Investment Education Seminar

While most are aware of the benefits derived from actively investing in the financial markets, many feel ill-equipped to manage their investments. This is primarily due to a lack of understanding and knowledge of the investment marketplace.

Our *"Invest Smarter,... Profit More"* Investment Education Seminar is comprehensive, detailed, and covers all fundamental aspects of investment education.

Subjects Covered:

Stocks	Bonds
Mutual Funds	Money Markets
Securities Markets	Securities Analysis
Margin	Options

...and much more...

This seminar is interactive, combining questions and answers intertwined with the lecture presentation. We believe this format enhances the learning process by providing an active and interesting approach to teaching investment fundamentals.

Because class size is extremely important to the learning process, seating is very limited. All seminars will be held on Saturdays only, from 9am - 4pm.

WHY WAIT,.. Register Today and **reserve your space.**

1 Registrant = $199.99   2 Registrants = $169.99* 3 or more Registrants = $139.99*
*Multiple registrations must be paid with one payment. (Prices subject to change)

For More information or to **Pre-Register for Free**

visit
www .FinancialEducation.org

Our "Live" or "Virtual" seminar is the perfect compliment to our "Home-Study" investment education course.

Appendix

Speech by SEC Chairman:
Expanding the Promise of Opportunity and Security Through Saving and Investing

Arthur
Levitt

Former
SEC
Chairman

Remarks by **Arthur Levitt**

Chairman, U.S. Securities & Exchange Commission

Before the Consumer Federation of America, Washington, D.C.

December 3, 1998

Thank you very much for your warm welcome. I want to thank Katie for her generous introduction. It is a great pleasure to be with you all today. This conference – and more importantly, your efforts to better inform America's investors – recognize one undeniable truth of our time: an era of institutional reliance is ending; **an era of self-reliance has begun.**

Today, more and more of us are taking responsibility for our own retirement needs. In the process, savings and investment habits have been dramatically transformed. More Americans invest in the stock market than ever before. More than one in three American families now invests in mutual funds – that's more than 35 million households. Fund assets, at around $4.9 trillion, now exceed insured commercial bank deposits, which stand at $2.4 trillion.

Back when most of us saved at a bank, bought whole life insurance, or had a defined benefit plan, the responsibility for investment decisions was in someone else's hands. But that's no longer true. By entering the less certain world of our capital markets, more than 50 million American investors have assumed higher risk in the hope of higher reward.

This change did not happen overnight; indeed, it's been the better part of a century in the making. Wall Street was practically a private club until World War I. The war effort was credited by the first SEC Chairman with creating "a vast number of security holders. From a few hundred thousand before 1916 who held securities, more than 20 million became investors during the War, mostly in bonds."

As dramatic a change as this was, it involved government bonds, which are among the most secure investments. Americans by and large continued to shun the stock markets, and the Depression served to reinforce that risk-averse philosophy.

For decade after decade, Americans were conservative savers focused on keeping money in federally insured bank accounts and maintaining life insurance.

This transformation in how and where Americans save and invest has enormous implications for our markets, our economy and our society. **The plain truth is that there is an unacceptably wide gap between financial knowledge and financial responsibilities**. If every investor in this country knew the fundamentals of saving and investing, we might be talking about a completely different subject today. But we know we don't have that luxury.

You know the challenges we face as well as I do. **Tens of millions of Americans lack the basic saving and investing information they need to prepare for retirement or to meet other financial goals**. More than half of all Americans have never even tried to figure how much money they'll need to save for retirement.

Too many people don't know how to assess the risks of different financial products. Too many people don't know how to choose an investment, or investment professional, or where to turn for help. **While 63 percent know the difference between a halfback and a quarterback, only 12 percent know the difference between a load and no-load mutual fund.** Millions don't understand the purpose of diversification. Millions have market expectations that are totally out of line with historic averages.   Is there any doubt that we are in the midst of a financial literacy crisis?

Earlier this year, the SEC, the Consumer Federation of America and a national coalition of government agencies, business groups, and other consumer organizations launched the *Facts on Saving and Investing Campaign.*

Our goal is to motivate Americans to get the facts they need to achieve financial security and avoid costly mistakes. Even if the government had all of the resources and power in the world to protect investors, I know there is no better way to prevent fraud and abuse than to educate investors. But, this campaign is not only about improving investor knowledge. That's half the battle. Earlier, I stated that more Americans than ever are investing in the stock market. We know that we need to reach out to these new investors to help ensure they understand the relationship between risk and return and the benefits of a diversified portfolio.

We know that this is a critical element of making suitable and sound investments at the right time in their lives.

But, what about the tens of millions of Americans who aren't investing in the stock market. **What about the 90 percent of Americans who could contribute to an IRA, but don't? What about the one-third of Americans who could participate in a retirement plan, but fail to do so?** Plainly put, what about those Americans who simply aren't saving? Just last month, the Commerce Department reported that **Americans personal savings rate for October was in negative territory – minus 0.2%.** I was saddened to learn that's the lowest it's been since the Great Depression.

I have cited a lot of stats. Few, however, trouble me more than this one which the CFA uncovered: sixty-five million American households will probably fail to realize one or more of their major life goals because they have not developed a basic financial plan.

As you know, these Americans are some of our country's more vulnerable citizens. Shouldn't it be incumbent upon every one of us to get across to all Americans – from every income level – **that saving early and investing over the long-term is not only smart and sound, but increasingly necessary?** Shouldn't a lower-wage worker hear the importance of saving and investing just as often as the recent college graduate? Shouldn't a worker in a textile factory know how much he or she needs to save to retire comfortably just as much as a worker in a high-tech company?

I realize I'm preaching to the choir. I know Senator Metzenbaum, Steve Brobeck and Barbara Roper have made the importance of saving and investing for all Americans a clear and unambiguous goal of the Consumer Federation of America. As we move forward, the efforts of consumer groups will play an indispensable role in educating more Americans about their retirement options.

One doesn't have to be an expert on the consumer-interest movement to recognize the influence it has had on our lives. Whether looking for a dependable car or a safe toy for our kids, the right health plan or the right foods, the consumer movement has made all of our lives better.

But, I have noticed that many consumer groups have traditionally stayed away from financial services issues. This is not all that surprising. In the past, our capital markets have been viewed as the sole province of the wealthy. **But today, it has never been more clear that investing and saving for one's retirement is just as much a pocket book issue as buying a car.**

I invite other consumer-interest groups to join the Facts on Saving and Investing Campaign in spreading the message about saving and investing. Your voice and those of other consumer groups can play a critical role in helping America's workers to take control of their financial futures. And, it has never been more important than now.

I believe that history will view the later part of this decade and the beginning of the next as a time when one of the greatest influx of new and inexperienced investors entered our markets. The proliferation of defined contribution plans and new technology, no doubt, will continue to bring many new investors into the market.

But, I fear that the range of investment and savings options may confuse and overwhelm many current as well as potential investors. Choosing among thousands of stocks, bonds, funds, and insurance products can be a daunting task. **<u>Before we ask Americans to make informed investment decisions, they need to know three things – what are their investment goals, when will they need the money, and how much risk can they afford</u>**. Only then can they choose investments that match their objectives.

Consider the influence of the Internet. Today, an average individual investor has more power and information available at his fingertips than ever before. Investors now have ready access to information that up until a few years ago was available only to securities professionals.
And, the amount of information available on the Internet is simply mind-boggling. Indeed, if you were to click through ten new financial Web sites a day, you could keep going for two and a half years before exhausting the possibilities. And those are just the sites posted in English.

Turn on the T.V. or the radio, open a newspaper – and you will see advertisements for mutual funds – each with their own 5-star rating and two, three, four or five-year performance histories. How many of you have seen advertisements for the growing number of Internet stock trading services? Turn to any of the financial channels and you will find a pundit talking about earnings forecasts for company X and breaking news about company Y. Is any of us really surprised that many potential investors don't know where to begin?

During my years on Wall Street and at the Commission, I have learned one all-important lesson: ask questions. And if you are not satisfied or still confused, ask more questions. If every saver and investor in this country inquired, peppered, or even annoyed someone in the position to answer questions, I have no doubt that many more people out there would be meeting their financial goals and not lose their hard earned dollars to fraud and abuse.

Together, we need to give people the tools to ask the right questions and get the right answers. How do we do it? I think there are three things we should do:

First, has anyone here heard about the importance of saving from either listening to the radio or watching T.V.? We've all heard the important warning that "friends don't let friends drive drunk." But we never hear that "friends don't let friends squander their financial future." We should hear *that* message on the radio and T.V.

Second, companies should take a greater role in teaching their workers about money. Employers that provide financial literacy programs are more than repaid through higher worker morale, greater productivity, and lower employee turnover.

Third, I applaud the efforts of our partners to expand financial literacy instruction in the schools. This spring, from April 25 to May 1st, many partners in the Facts on Saving and Investing Campaign will showcase their school programs. They will encourage partners to visit classrooms across the country to get students and young adults excited about saving for tomorrow. Let's not graduate one more generation that hasn't learned the financial facts of life.

Today, we stand at what may be a defining moment in American economic history. This may someday be described as the era of democratization of American finance. **But, if the vast majority of investors are not informed and not educated, opportunity will lose out to ignorance.**

We don't have a second to waste. The time to act is now. If you sense some urgency in my voice, it's for good reason. As some of you may know, a few weeks ago, I discussed the implications of investing Social Security in the stock market.

Clearly, we are all concerned about closing the knowledge gap that exists among investors today. But, it becomes even more of an imperative if we adopt individual accounts as part of Social Security reform. **With individual accounts, more than 140 million American workers would be investing their retirement funds in securities**.

Increased risk, through greater choice, holds the potential for greater returns. That's the upside of a system of individual accounts. The downside is that uninformed investors often won't be in a position to capture that potential. They risk making poor decisions, perhaps through ignorance or because they fall prey to fraudulent advice or misleading sales practices.

Whatever may happen, one thing is certain: the face of our financial system is changing and will continue to change. And, more and more of those changes are being driven to meet investor's needs. Take our Plain English initiative as an example. Today, when a prospectus or other investor document is submitted to the SEC for comment, one of our foremost considerations is whether it accurately and effectively communicates with investors. In the last two years, through a cooperative effort with the industry, we've been successful in setting a new standard of clarity.

The unmistakable trend in investor communication is away from impenetrable masses of linguistic underbrush – in favor of economy and accessibility.

Years ago, the problem was a lack of information; today, it is a glut of information. Prospectuses have to work for investors, if they are to thrive in the new world of information. And, with the influx of new investors, we have to concentrate on connecting people with the great volume of information that's out there.

I see Plain English as an example of the type of positive change that comes from a wider circle of participation in our capital markets. If the number of investors had stayed relatively static over the last decade, consumer-driven interest to spur change like this would have been rare. And, companies would feel far less pressure to improve their communication with the investing public.

* *

Today, we have a unique opportunity before us: to help generations of Americans make the most of their God given potential. Whether one person actively saves and invests or another fails to put away one penny, they both, fundamentally, share the same goals.

Who would argue that every American worker doesn't want to retire comfortably? Who would argue that a parent doesn't want to be able to send their child to college? Who would argue that any person doesn't want to provide the health and security every family deserves? No one would.

We should always remember that most people don't invest just for the thrill of getting in on the hottest new IPO. Most people don't buy one stock in the morning and sell it in the afternoon. Most people aren't betting that bond yields will fall during a certain time period.

Most people invest and save for a very simple, but immeasurably important reason: **to safeguard their retirement years, the futures of their children and their children's children.**

America has always guaranteed opportunity for anybody willing to work for it. **But, if people don't invest and save over the course of a lifetime, they deny themselves security and opportunity**.

That's a tragedy. Working together, I can't think of any more important mission than reaching out to every person in this great country and offering opportunity through education; empowerment through participation; and security through responsibility.

I look forward to joining with you all as we work towards these goals.

Thank you very much.

www.ingramcontent.com/pod-product-compliance
Lightning Source LLC
Chambersburg PA
CBHW081508200326
41518CB00015B/2429